Twenty
TYRANTS

Alan Blackwood

Illustrated by Edward Mortelmans

Twenty Names

Twenty Names in Art
Twenty Names in Aviation
Twenty Campaigners for Change
Twenty Names in Classical Music
Twenty Names in Crime
Twenty Explorers
Twenty Names in Film
Twenty Inventors
Twenty Names in Medicine
Twenty Names in Modern Literature
Twenty Novelists
Twenty Names in Pop Music
Twenty Names in Space Exploration
Twenty Names in Sport
Twenty Names in Theatre
Twenty Tyrants

Editor: Rosemary Ashley

First published in 1989 by
Wayland (Publishers Limited)
61 Western Road, Hove
East Sussex BN3 1JD, England

British Library Cataloguing in Publication Data
Blackwood, Alan, *1932* –
   Twenty tyrants. – (Twenty names).
   1. Heads of state & rulers, history –
   Biographies – Collections
   I. Title   II. Series   909

   ISBN 1–85210–140–7

Phototypeset by Kalligraphics Ltd, Horley, Surrey
Printed in Italy by G. Canale C.S.p.A., Turin
Bound in Britain at The Bath Press, Avon

Contents

Power and oppression

The dictionary definition of a tyrant is 'an oppressive or cruel ruler'. We might also say that a tyrant is someone who is feared by others. Both descriptions perfectly suit the twenty characters featured in this book. In other ways, however, they are by no means alike. The Roman Emperor Nero simply wanted to enjoy himself. The Renaissance general Cesare Borgia, by contrast, was an utterly ruthless man, whose only aim in life, at whatever the cost, was to wield power and domination over others. Tomas de Torquemada and Maximilien Robespierre were fanatics, who believed that what they were doing was right and for the good of all. Others again, such as Henry VIII and Catherine the Great, had good intentions, but were changed for the worse by events. A few, above all Adolf Hitler, altered the whole course of history.

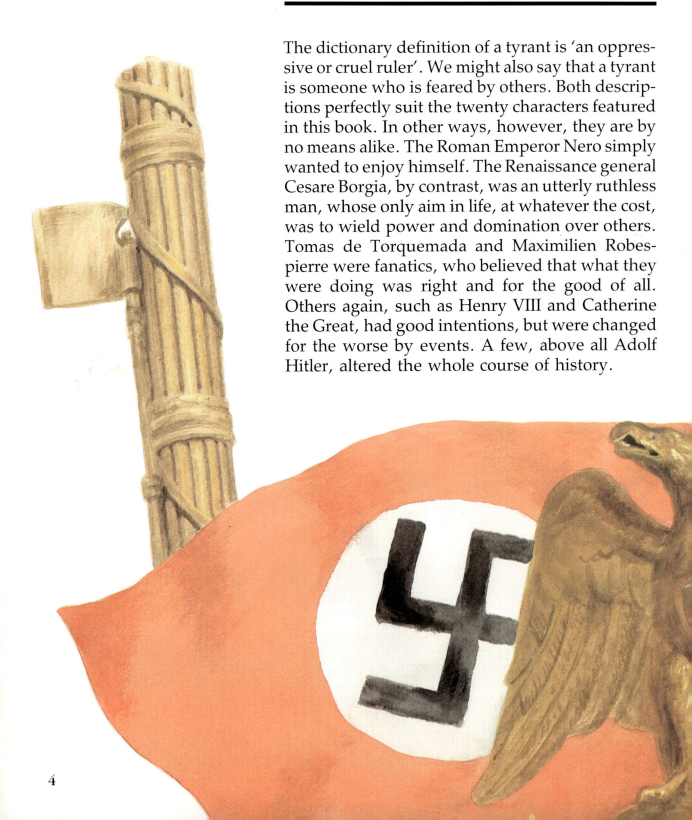

All these men and women are fascinating to read about, as wicked or corrupt people often are. And the fact that they have belonged to almost every race or nation of the world, from Biblical times to the present day, means that by reading about them we are also learning a good deal about world history.

The most intriguing question of all is why did they become tyrants. A famous historian once said that power tends to corrupt, and absolute power corrupts absolutely. The people in this book prove him right. The terrible things some of them did came from the abuse of too much power. Nor should we speak only of the past. As we read in the cases of, for example, Idi Amin and Pol Pot, tyrants are still with us. If there is a lesson for us in all this, it is that such democratic principles as free elections, justice according to the law, religious and political freedom, put a limit on personal power, and so protect us from the rule of tyrants.

1

Emperor Ch'in Shih-Huang-Ti

The Great Wall of China is one of the wonders of the world. It stretches across northern China for a distance of over 2,700 kilometres. Most of it was built at the command of the Emperor Ch'in Shih-Huang-Ti, the first ruler of all China.

He came to the throne of the powerful northern province of Ch'in (corresponding to the present-day provinces of Kansu and Shensi) when he was only thirteen years old, but soon began a series of savage wars against the other Chinese provinces. That is how he came to be the first Emperor of China.

To protect his domains from the Mongols and other warlike races of central Asia, he decided to extend and strengthen the fortified wall, portions of which had already been built. To finish the task as quickly as possible, he conscripted a work-

c259BC born in the old Chinese province of Ch'in
246BC inherits the throne of Ch'in province
237–221BC conquers almost all of China
220BC directs building of the Great Wall of China
210BC dies while touring his provinces

Right *Stone by stone and brick by brick, the Great Wall of China was built. Thousands perished at the task.*

6

force of over a million men. The wall was continued over mountains and across deserts, and the work went on in the blazing heat of summer and freezing winter cold. Thousands perished from sickness and exhaustion, their bodies being buried where they fell, in the wall's foundations or bricked up in the wall itself.

But like many tyrannical rulers, the Emperor Ch'in also lived in fear. His imperial palace had thousands of rooms, and he made a habit of sleeping in a different one each night, in case anyone was planning to murder him in his bed. He was even afraid of what might happen to him when he died. He had an enormous mausoleum built, and filled it with an army of life-sized terracotta soldiers, armed with real swords, spears, bows and arrows, which he hoped would protect his body and soul from evil spirits. When this mausoleum was recently re-discovered and excavated, its contents caused a world-wide sensation.

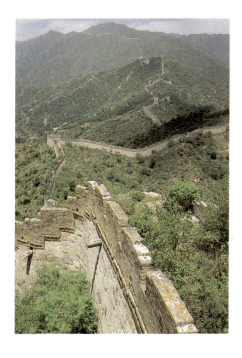

Above *The Great Wall of China as it is today – one of the world's greatest tourist attractions.*

2

Herod The Great

The mighty Roman Empire was, of course, governed from the capital city of Rome. But the rulers of Rome needed the help of local kings and princes in the running of such a huge empire. The Jewish King Herod the Great was one of those who helped the Roman rulers.

He began his career as Governor of Galilee, in the region of Palestine. Then the victorious Roman General Octavius (later Augustus Caesar) promoted him King of the neighbouring province of Judea, which was the homeland of the Jews.

Herod enlarged the territory of Judea. He ordered the restoration of the great Temple in Jerusalem and the construction of many splendid new buildings. However, he did all this simply to establish his own power. He cared nothing for the rights and customs of the Jewish people, and they hated him for his injustice and cruelty.

King Herod orders the arrest of his wife. Like most tyrants, he trusted no one, not even his own family .

Afraid for his own safety, Herod recruited an army of foreign mercenaries to form a strong police force, and he had many Jews arrested and executed. He even ordered the killing of his own wife and three of his sons, because he suspected them of plotting against him.

Herod is best remembered today from the account of him in the Bible. According to St Matthew's Gospel, Herod was told of the birth of the infant Jesus in Bethlehem by the Three Wise Men. Remembering also the prophecies that spoke of a Messiah (Divine Leader) to lead the Jewish people, Herod tried to find out where the child lay, in order to kill him. Jesus, meanwhile, had been taken by his parents, Mary and Joseph, for safety to Egypt. Herod, when he realized how he had been tricked, flew into a terrible rage and ordered the massacre of all infant male children up to the age of two years, who were living in or near Bethlehem.

c73BC born in southern Palestine
c40BC appointed King of Judea by Octavius
c4BC dies in his palace, probably insane

3
Queen Boudicca

Queen Boudicca (or Boadicea as she is sometimes known) is a heroine to the British. Her story is also a grim lesson in the way injustice and cruelty breeds even worse crimes.

At the time when most of Britain was a part of the Roman Empire, there was a British tribe called the Iceni. They were ruled by King Prasutagus and his Queen Boudicca, and they lived quite amicably with their Roman overlords. But when King Prasutagus died, the local Roman governor behaved very badly towards the Iceni, claiming their East Anglian homeland for himself, and demanding huge taxes. When Queen Boudicca protested, he had her stripped and flogged.

In a fury, Boudicca led the Iceni in open revolt against the Romans. At the head of an army of wild tribesmen, she attacked the towns of Camulodunum (Colchester), Verulamium (St Albans) and Londinium (London), burning them

Right *Queen Boudicca is stripped and flogged by the Romans.*

CAD20 born in East Anglia in South East England
AD40 leads revolt of the Iceni tribe against the Romans
AD62 defeated in battle by the Romans and probably commits suicide

to the ground, and killing all their inhabitants. For British women who had married Roman men, she reserved even more hideous punishments.

A Roman chronicler has left us with this vivid description of the avenging queen. 'She was very big and fierce looking, with a great mass of red hair falling down her back. She wore a golden necklace and a tunic of many colours, and brandished a spear, to strike fear into all who saw her.'

Boudicca's revolt, though, did not last long. The bulk of the Roman army in Britain, which had been campaigning in North Wales, came hurrying south. Boudicca's disorderly soldiers, armed only with slings and spears, were no match for the disciplined ranks of the Roman legions, and in a battle somewhere north of London (nobody is sure of the exact place), they were annihilated. Nobody is sure either what happened to Boudicca herself, but it is believed she escaped from the battle, and then took poison and died.

Above *An engraving showing Queen Boudicca raising her army, which took terrible revenge on the Romans.*

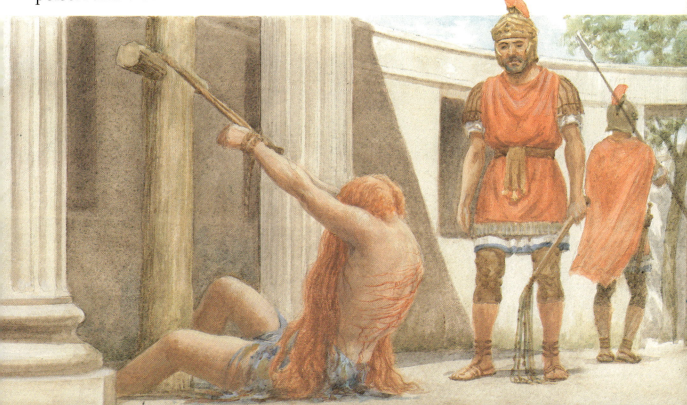

4
Emperor Nero

The Roman Empire lasted for over five hundred years. At its greatest, it stretched all the way from Egypt in the south, to the British Isles in the north, and from Spain in the west, to the Caspian Sea in the east. It was governed, sometimes by a Senate (or parliament), sometimes by army generals. The first ruler to be named Emperor was Augustus Caesar, who made the capital of Rome the greatest city in the world, with a system of roads leading to it from all parts of the Empire. Not all the emperors who followed him were as great or good. One very bad emperor was Nero.

Nero became emperor when he succeeded his stepfather Claudius. To make sure of his position, he murdered both his mother and his wife, whom he suspected might plot against him. He then settled down to a life of idleness and pleasure, instead of attending to the government of the Empire. He considered himself a fine actor and

AD34 born near Rome
AD54 succeeds his father Claudius as Emperor of Rome
AD64 Rome badly damaged by fire, prompting Nero's persecution of the Christians
AD68 deposed by generals backed by the Senate, and commits suicide

musician, and commanded people to attend his performances. From all accounts, he was not very talented, though no one ever dared to tell him so.

The worst period of his reign followed a disastrous fire that destroyed many of Rome's great monuments. Nero, we are told, put the blame on the Christians. They were already causing trouble in parts of the Empire, and it was easy to whip up anger and resentment against them. He had many of them arrested and sacrificed to wild animals in the appalling blood sports held in the Roman Coliseum.

Above *An old print showing Christians being torn apart by wild animals in Nero's Rome.*

Nero also demanded that high taxes should be raised throughout the provinces, to pay for the rebuilding of Rome and these taxes were a cause of much discontent throughout the Empire.

Some historians argue that the Emperor Nero was not nearly such a bad man as he is usually reported to have been. Nevertheless, a group of generals finally led a revolt against him, and he committed suicide.

Below *Nero lounges in his palace, leading a life of pleasure and luxury. But he could be a ruthless tyrant when it suited him.*

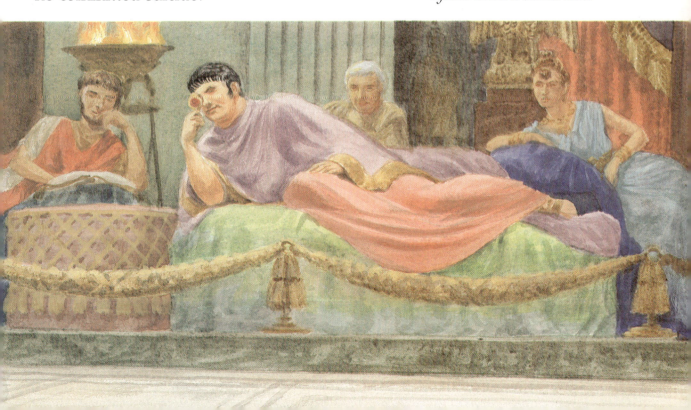

5
Attila the Hun

The decline and break-up of the Roman Empire was hastened by the invasions of various warlike tribes and races known as the Barbarians. One of the fiercest of these were the Huns. They were wild, brilliant horsemen, and they rode into Europe from central Asia. At the same time, they joined forces with the Vandals, Ostrogoths, Franks and other Barbarian tribesmen from Russia, Scandinavia and north Germany. The Hun leader, Attila, united them all into one huge and terrifying horde.

Attila the Hun was known as 'The Scourge of God', meaning a terrible kind of punishment. He first attacked the Byzantine Empire, which had been founded in south-eastern Europe in AD 330, by the Roman Emperor Constantine after he was converted to Christianity. Attila's hordes killed thousands of defenceless people and laid waste to their lands, forcing the Byzantine emperor to pay him huge sums of money.

Still hungry for bloody conquest, Attila turned his forces westward, sweeping across Germany and on into the Roman province of Gaul (France), until they were checked by a hastily assembled Roman army in a desperate battle near the present-day town of Châlons-sur-Marne.

Attila retreated to Hungary, gathered more Barbarians to his side, and launched a new and even more terrible campaign southward over the Alps and into Italy, the very heart of the Roman Empire. Fire, famine and death marked his progress, as he rode on south towards Rome itself. In fact, it was probably only a lack of food that stopped him short of the city.

Attila temporarily withdrew, and was planning another campaign against Rome when he died. Deprived of his leadership, his army broke up, the Huns rode back into Asia, and a chapter of terror and destruction was over for the people of Europe.

c406	born somewhere in Asia
433	proclaimed King of the Huns
447	attacks the Byzantine Empire
451	attacks Gaul but is repulsed at Châlons-sur-Marne
452	invades Italy and advances on Rome
453	dies while planning a new campaign in Italy

Emissaries from the emperor offer Attila a fortune of gold, after his hordes have overrun the Byzantine Empire.

15

6
Genghis Khan

Another conqueror from the vast lands of Asia was Genghis Khan. When he was born he was given the name of Temujin. He was still only a boy when his father, a local Mongol chieftan, was murdered. Young Temujin had to learn quickly how to protect himself and become a tough and ruthless leader. Defeating all his rivals for power, he then united the nomadic Mongol tribes of Siberia, and at their holy meeting place of Karakorum, on the edge of the Himalayan mountains, was proclaimed Great Khan or Chief. He then took the title of Genghis Khan, meaning 'Mighty King'.

His Mongol horsemen, like the Huns before them, were incredibly tough, short, stocky men, and the shaggy little horses they rode were just as tough and strong. Together, they were all but invincible. Genghis Khan first led his wild horsemen east and south into China, capturing the

c1167 born in Mongolia
c1180 becomes Mongol leader and takes the title Genghis Khan
1211–15 conquers northern China
1218–22 conquers Afghanistan, Persia and southern Russia
1227 dies fighting in China

Right *Genghis Khan about to excecute a prisoner. Although he was a cruel and violent ruler, he brought law and order to his huge empire.*

capital, Peking. Leaving one of his trusted lieutenants in command, he headed west across the deserts and mountains of central Asia to Afghanistan and Persia (Iran) as far as the Black Sea, destroying everyone who tried to stop him, including the fierce and bloodthirsty Turks.

Thus Genghis Khan created an empire that stretched for nearly 7,000 kilometres, from the shores of the Pacific Ocean almost into Europe. He was a tyrannical ruler; but he also issued a proper code of laws, called the Yassa. With his sons, he maintained law and order through his vast domains, by building roads and organizing a kind of military postal service, through which he issued his commands.

Genghis Khan was killed while putting down a rebellion in northern China; but his grandson, Kublai Khan, founded the Mongol or Yuan dynasty in China, which so amazed the Venetian explorer Marco Polo when he journeyed there in 1275.

Above *The wild landscape of Mongolia, heartland of Genghis Khan's empire.*

7
Tomas de Torquemada

The fifteenth century was an exciting time for Spain. King Ferdinand and Queen Isabella united the country and gave their backing to Christopher Columbus, whose voyage across the Atlantic Ocean led to the discovery of the Americas and the establishment of Spain's great overseas empire.

But it was not a happy time for everyone. The land had earlier been occupied by the Moors of North Africa, who were Muslims. There was also a large Jewish population. Queen Isabella, a deeply religious woman, decided that everybody in Spain must now become a Christian, or leave the country. The man she employed to help her make Spain a devout Christian country was Tomas de Torquemada. He was a Spanish monk, whose devotion to Christianity had already pleased the Pope in Rome. He seemed the ideal man for the job.

Torquemada, however, did not just try to convert

Below *A suspected heretic is interrogated at a tribunal of the Spanish Inquisition.*

Muslims and Jews to Christianity. He was appointed Inquisitor-General, with authority to inquire into the religious beliefs and practices of everyone in Spain. He was especially concerned with matters of heresy – ideas or beliefs that were in any way different from the official teaching of the Pope and the established Church. Torquemada could arrest anybody whom he suspected of heresy, witchcraft, or any other 'crime' against the Church. Most frightening of all was the authority given to Torquemada to torture suspects, in order to make them 'confess' to their crimes.

Torquemada and his colleagues of the Inquisition believed they were doing a good and necessary job, defending Christianity and the Church against evil. In fact, thousands of innocent and harmless people were arrested, imprisoned and tortured; and if they were then found guilty of heresy or witchcraft at special courts or tribunals, they could be burnt at the stake. The Spanish Inquisition did not end with Torquemada. It lingered on for another three hundred years.

Above *A tribunal or court of the Inquisition in session.*

c1420 born in Torquemada,
       near Valladolid in Spain
1483 appointed Inquisitor-
       General by the Pope
1498 dies in Avila, Spain

8
Vlad Dracula

Everybody has heard of Count Dracula, the legendary vampire who rose from his tomb each night to feast upon the blood of the living. Not so many people know that there was once a real Count Dracula. The name means 'Son of the Dragon', and he ruled over the ancient province of Wallachia in eastern Europe, situated between the wild Transylvanian Alps and the River Danube, that is now a part of present-day Romania.

The period of Count Vlad Dracula's life and rule coincided with the capture of Constantinople by the Ottoman Turks in 1453. Wallachia stood as a kind of buffer state between the expanding Ottoman Empire and the Kingdom of Hungary; and some historians have portrayed the Count as a valiant warrior, who defended Christian Europe against the fierce Turkish invaders. This may be so, but there is plenty of evidence also of his appalling cruelty, both towards his enemies and his

Below *Count Vlad Dracula gloats over the dreadful fate awaiting another of his victims.*

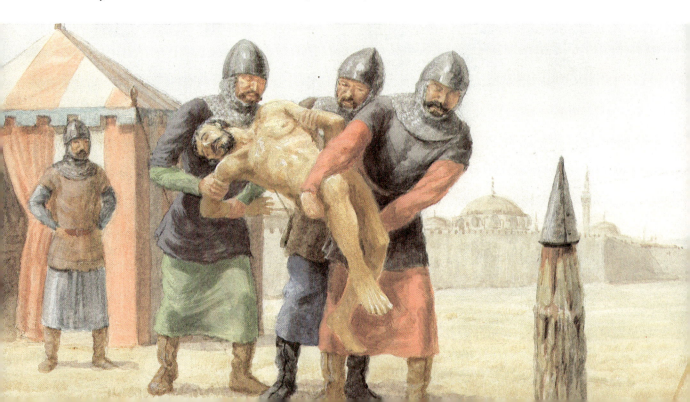

own people. His most usual method of punishment, for prisoners of war and anyone else whom he disliked, was to impale them on iron or wooden spikes. He put thousands to death in this gruesome way. There is also a story of how the Count rid the land of beggars and cripples by inviting them to a banquet. He then sealed all the doors and windows of the hall and burnt them alive. Yet another story concerns some Turkish messengers. When they failed to remove their turbans in his presence he had the offending headgear nailed to their skulls!

Nobody knows exactly when and how Count Dracula died. But printing had recently been invented, and accounts of his atrocities quickly spread his name across Europe. There was even an early printed woodcut, showing him greedily feasting on flesh among hundreds of impaled bodies. Such bloodthirsty stories and pictures have helped to create the myths and legends of human vampires.

Above *An early woodcut, showing Count Dracula surrounded by his victims.*

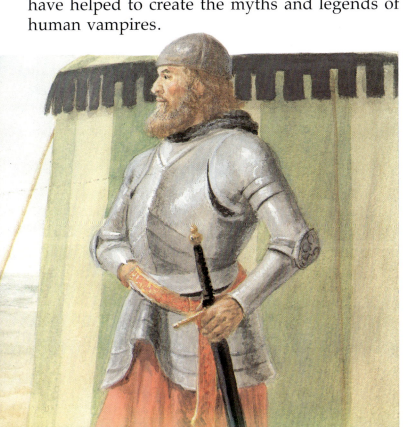

c1430 born in the Romanian province of Wallachia
c1460 leads an army against the invading Ottoman Turks
c1476 dies, perhaps assassinated or killed fighting the Turks

9
Cesare Borgia

Italy in Renaissance times produced some of the world's greatest artists, including Leonardo da Vinci and Michelangelo. It was also a very warlike place, largely governed by a number of rich and powerful families who were always quarrelling with each other. Among the strongest and most ruthless of these families were the Borgias; and their most notorious member was Prince Cesare Borgia.

His father was Pope Alexander VI. In those days the Pope held a very strong political position and Cesare himself was given the title of Cardinal when he was still only seventeen years old. Backed up by this influential position and with advice from his scheming father, Cesare Borgia aimed to beat all his rivals and become the most powerful man in Italy. 'Aut Caesar aut nihil' (Either Caesar or Nothing) was his motto, referring back to the days when the Caesars ruled

c1475 born in Rome, Italy
1492 appointed a cardinal by his father, Pope Alexander VI, and begins his ruthless career
1503 death of Pope Alexander leads to his own downfall
1507 killed in battle in Spain

Right *The grim end for one tyrant. Killed in battle, Cesare Borgia's mutilated body is discovered in a ravine.*

Imperial Rome. He arranged the murder of his own brother. He forced his sister Lucrezia into a number of marriages, solely for his own political advantage, then, when it was convenient to him, murdered one of her husbands. He carried out more political murders, mainly against the rival Orsini family. Having gained control of large parts of Italy, he terrorized the people with his large private army.

When Cesare Borgia's father Pope Alexander VI died, his enemies united against him, capturing and imprisoning him. He managed to escape, but was killed in battle soon after. His ruthless career inspired the celebrated Italian courtier and diplomat Niccolo Machiavelli, when he came to write *The Prince*, his famous book about the art and uses of politics. Machiavelli admired Cesare Borgia, believing that he was trying to unite Italy. But there is little doubt that he was interested only in himself, and would stop at nothing to get his own way.

Above *Lucrezia Borgia dancing before her father, Pope Alexander VI, and her brother Cesare.*

10
Henry VIII

When the English King Henry VIII came to the throne, aged eighteen, everybody in the land looked forward to a long and happy reign. The new young king was tall and athletic, loved languages, music and poetry, and was interested also in all the new scientific and philosophical ideas of the Renaissance age.

Things started to go wrong for him and for England when his first wife, Catherine of Aragon, failed to give him a son and heir to the throne. Henry wanted to divorce Catherine and marry again, but the Pope in Rome, who was then the religious head of the Church throughout most of Europe, would not agree to this. Henry then defied the Pope and married Anne Boleyn. He went further, and declared himself the Head of the Church in England. At the same time, he instructed his ruthless chief minister, Thomas Cromwell, to close down all the monasteries and

1491 born in Greenwich Palace, England
1509 crowned King of England
1527 the Pope refuses to grant Henry a divorce from Catherine of Aragon
1533 marries Anne Boleyn
1535 declares himself head of the Church in England and begins destruction of the monasteries
1536 orders the execution of Anne
1542 orders the execution of his fifth wife, Catherine Howard
1547 dies a sick man but feared by all

sell their lands. The monasteries, in England as elsewhere, were like churches, schools and hospitals combined; and by destroying them, King Henry destroyed a whole way of life, as well as many beautiful buildings and works of art.

As Henry grew older, his character and temperament changed for the worse. He dismissed one of his chief ministers, Cardinal Wolsey, and robbed him of his palace at Hampton Court, on the River Thames near London. He beheaded Sir Thomas More, another of his ministers, and two of his own six wives, Anne Boleyn and, after her, Catherine Howard. Many more people were executed or rotted in prison, if Henry suspected them of disloyalty or they failed to give him what he wanted.

By the time he died, King Henry was a fat and monstrous figure, feared by all. Although he left England a strong country, the religious disputes and divisions he had started were to bring misery and bloodshed to the land for years to come.

Above *A contemporary portrait of Henry VIII presiding over his court.*

Below *The King dismisses Cardinal Wolsey, who is mocked by the court jester.*

11
Ivan the Terrible

Russia in the sixteenth century was a land shrouded in mystery, almost unknown to the rest of Europe. The huge country of forest and rolling plain stretched on and on into Asia, its towns and villages separated by vast distances and often cut off from each other and from the rest of the world through the long, dark, snow-bound winters. Russia's large but scattered population of peasants (or serfs as they were called) was ruled over by ruthless, land-owning nobles or boyars.

This was the situation when the Grand Duke Ivan IV of Moscow was born. The infant Ivan was himself brought up by brutal boyars. But as soon as he was old enough, he decided to break their power, by declaring himself the first Tsar or Emperor of all Russia. To strengthen his position, he raised a large army and pushed Russia's territories deep into Asia beyond the Caspian

Sea. In the far north of the country, he built the port of Archangel, and when the English explorer and merchant Richard Chancellor sailed to Archangel, Ivan made a trade agreement with him.

All this helped to turn Russia into a great power. But the death of Ivan's wife seemed to have unhinged his mind, and all the violence he had experienced as a boy now came to the surface in his own behaviour. The treachery of one of his counsellors roused his suspicions, and he began to believe that he was surrounded by people plotting against him, including the Bishop of Moscow whom he had horribly strangled. In a fit of insane rage he struck and killed his own son. Most dreadful of all was Ivan's expedition against the lovely old Russian city of Novgorod. Because he suspected some local boyars of plotting against him, he rode to the city with his troops, set fire to every building in sight and massacred the entire population.

Above *The Tsar meets the English explorer Richard Chancellor, one of the happier episodes of his reign.*

1530	born in Moscow
1547	crowned as Ivan IV, Tsar of Russia
1550	begins a fruitful period of rule, extending Russia's frontiers and building the port of Archangel
1560	the death of his wife brings a change of character, and he commits many atrocities
1584	dies a cruel tyrant

Left *Tsar Ivan cradles his dying son in his arms, having just struck him a mortal blow in a fit of rage.*

27

12
Catherine the Great

Catherine the Great of Russia is sometimes described as a benevolent despot, meaning a ruler who uses power for the good of the people. However, in many ways, she became a tyrant.

Catherine was a German-born princess who was married to the heir to the Russian throne. Her husband, in fact, was a feeble young man; and soon after he was crowned Tsar she had him deposed and murdered, then reigned as Empress or Tsarina in his place. Two years later she arranged for the murder of the young Tsar Ivan VI who, as a child, had been deposed and thrown into prison by his aunt Empress Elizabeth I.

These crimes seem to have made her contemptuous of men. All her life, Catherine used them, as lovers or ministers, then cast them aside. Indeed, she proved to be much tougher than most men.

Catherine did achieve some good things. She reformed the administration of government. She

1729	born a princess in Germany
1762	deposes and murders her Russian husband, Tsar Peter III, and rules in his place
1764	has the rightful Tsar, Ivan VI, murdered in his prison
1772	fights her most successful campaign against Poland
1774	crushes a peasant revolt led by the Cossack chief Pugachev
1796	dies after thirty-four years as Tsarina

Right *The Empress Catherine and her favorite general, Field Marshal Potemkin, plan the conquest of the Crimea. Russia became a great empire during her long reign.*

also wished to improve conditions for the serfs, who were little better than slaves. She was interested in philosophy, and corresponded with the great French thinker and writer Voltaire.

But as her long reign continued, Catherine became harder and more ruthless. Instead of helping the serfs, she acted mercilessly against them when a Cossack chief, Emil Pugachev, led them in revolt. Her main ambition was to build up the Russian Empire. She fought two wars against Turkey, gaining new territory for Russia in the Caucasus Mountains and the Crimea. She also waged war against neighbouring Poland, grabbing more and more of its land, until the country virtually disappeared from the map.

There are stories that when Catherine the Great toured her provinces, carpenters hastily erected the facades of whole streets of wooden houses They looked clean and prosperous from her coach. It was felt that the important thing was to please her, otherwise there might be trouble!

Above *A contemporary painting of the Empress in all her power and glory.*

13
Maximilien Robespierre

On 14 July 1789, a large and angry crowd attacked and destroyed the old Bastille prison in Paris. It was a signal for people all over France to join the Revolution against the monarchy and the land-owning aristocracy. The French Revolution achieved a great deal in a short space of time. Its leaders redistributed land among the people, gave them more food, and created democratic forms of government. But the monarchs and govern-ments of other countries opposed revolutionary France, and the country was soon threatened with war and invasion. This opened the way for extremists like Maximilien Robespierre.

Robespierre was a leading member of the revolutionary Society of Friends of the Constitution, known as the Jacobins. He was among those who accused the French King Louis XVI and Queen Marie-Antoinette of treachery after they

Right *Another of Robespierre's victims faces the guillotine. These instruments of death were installed in many French towns and cities during his 'Reign of Terror'.*

1758	born near Arras, France
1789	elected to the new Constituent Assembly in Paris
1793	heads the Committee of Public Safety and instigates the Reign of Terror
1794	arrested and executed

had tried to escape from France, and demanded their execution. Then he gained control of the Committee of Public Safety, a kind of secret police force, formed to protect the security of the new French Republic. This gave him the power to arrest and execute almost anyone he chose.

For about a year, Robespierre was the virtual dictator of France, imprisoning and sending thousands to their death by guillotine, a new and horribly efficient method of execution, named after its inventor. Like all fanatics, Robespierre believed that what he was doing was absolutely right and good. But to everybody else, his period of rule was known as 'The Reign of Terror'.

Finally, a group of other revolutionary leaders, fearful for their own lives, had him arrested. Robespierre tried to commit suicide but was prevented from doing so. He soon followed all his own victims to the guillotine. With his death, the 'Reign of Terror' mercifully came to an end.

Above *The storming of the Bastille, the event that started the French Revolution, in July 1789.*

14
Benito Mussolini

Benito Mussolini, a tough and arrogant man, was born in Italy at the end of the nineteenth century, but he looked back to the days of the Roman Empire, when his country had ruled over the Western world. His political party took its name of Fascist from the ancient Roman emblem of authority – an axe in a bundle of sticks. Mussolini believed that respect for individual rights and freedoms were signs of weakness. For him, strength and power were the most important qualities.

Soon after the end of the First World War (1914–18), which had left Italy in a weak state politically, Mussolini and his Fascists, or Blackshirts as they were also known, staged a dramatic march on Rome, the capital of Italy, with the aim of overthrowing the government and taking power. They succeeded in their aim, and although there was still a king of Italy, Mussolini established himself

Below *Mussolini addressing the crowds from the balcony of his headquarters in Rome.*

as the country's ruler. He declared himself 'Il Duce' (The Leader), and became the first dictator of modern times.

Mussolini did improve the running of the country, building new factories and providing new land for farmers. It was said of him that he made the trains run on time! But his real aim was the creation of a new Roman Empire. His army and air force first conquered the helpless African country of Abyssinia (now Ethiopia). Then he joined his fellow dictator Adolf Hitler in a political and military 'Axis', hoping that a powerful Germany would help him win new conquests. Thus he brought Italy into the Second World War.

This was a terrible mistake. Italy was invaded by the Allies, and in 1943 Mussolini was deposed. He was rescued by Hitler, but was finally captured by Communist partisans, shot, and hung up by the heels in a square in Milan. Such was the end of the man who had brought ruin to his country through ruthless ambition and vanity.

Above *Il Duce, as Mussolini termed himself, raises his arm in the Fascist salute. He was a vain man who enjoyed making speeches.*

1883	born in the Romagna region of Italy
1922	leads a march of his Fascist Party on Rome and becomes prime minister, soon dictator
1935	invades Abyssinia
1940	declares war on Britain and France
1943	deposed and imprisoned, but rescued by the Germans
1945	captured by Italian Communist partisans and shot

15
Adolf Hitler

Adolf Hitler was born in Austria and first scraped a living in Vienna selling sketches in the street and doing odd jobs. He served in the German Army in the First World War, and after Germany's defeat in 1918, he saw his opportunity to gain power.

After the war Hitler made speeches, stirring up hatred against Jewish businessmen and communists, whom he blamed for the defeat of Germany and Austria. In 1921 he created a political party, the Nazi Party. In 1933, due largely to mass unemployment and ruinous inflation, Hitler and his Nazis were elected to power. He quickly banned all other political parties and trade unions, and, following Mussolini's example in Italy, he declared himself the one and only Leader or 'Führer' of the German state. He was aided by his propaganda minister, Joseph Goebbels, who controlled the newspapers, radio and cinema, and by the creation of the dreaded Gestapo, or secret police.

1889 born in Braunau, Austria
1914–18 serves in the German army in the First World War
1921 forms the Nazi Party
1923 imprisoned, and writes his political creed, *Mein Kampf* (My Struggle)
1933 becomes German Chancellor, then dictator
1939–45 leads Germany through the Second World War, committing suicide as the Soviet Red Army captures Berlin

Right *'Jew-baiting' in Hitler's Germany. Jews had to wear yellow stars, and they and their property were attacked by Nazi thugs. Many ordinary Germans seemed unaffected by such scenes.*

Hitler believed the Germans were part of a superior master race, and he aimed to unite Germany with Austria and other German-speaking territories into one all-powerful Reich, or State. He also set up concentration camps, run by a brutal branch of the army called the SS, where millions of Jews and people of other so-called inferior races were to be imprisoned and slaughtered.

Hitler's warlike actions so alarmed other nations that Britain and France finally declared war on the German Reich in 1939, and the Second World War began. Hitler's armed forces were at first everywhere victorious, and for a few years he ruled over most of Europe. But in June 1941 he invaded the huge Soviet Union (to him a hated communist state), and later that year the United States entered the war against him. Hitler's Reich, intended to last for a thousand years, was defeated in 1945, and he shot himself in a bunker in Berlin. He left behind more death, misery and ruin than any other person in history.

Above *Hitler in 1940, at the height of his power, inspects his troops.*

16
Joseph Stalin

Stalin means 'Man of Steel'. It was the name adopted by Joseph Dzugashvili, and it suited him only too well.

He was born in the province of Georgia, near the Caucasus Mountains, in what was still the old Imperial Russian Empire. He joined Lenin in the Bolshevik Revolution of 1917, which overthrew the rule of the Tsars and established the Soviet Union, the world's first Communist state.

When Lenin died in 1924, Stalin quickly established his position as virtual dictator of the Soviet Union. He then decided, as quickly as possible, to turn the nation from the old-fashioned agricultural country it had been under the Tsars into a modern industrial state. His policy of 'collectivization' forced millions of peasants into what amounted to slave labour. Many of them died. At the same time, Stalin tightened his grip on every other aspect of the nation's life. He eliminated all political rivals in the Communist Party in what were called purges – having them

1879	born in the Russian province of Georgia
1904	exiled to Siberia for political crimes
1917	takes a leading part in the Bolshevik Revolution
1924	succeeds Lenin as Soviet leader
1941–5	leads the Soviet Union to victory against Nazi Germany
1953	dies in office

Right *Stalin's secret police make an arrest during one of his political purges. His victims were either shot, or sent to Siberian prison camps, from which they rarely returned.*

executed or sent to labour camps in the far, freezing wastes of Siberia, where most of them perished. Writers, artists and composers too, lived in fear of him. If he felt that their work undermined his regime in any way, they could face exile to Siberia, labour camps or execution.

The industry that Stalin had built up, at such a dreadful price, did enable the Soviet Union eventually, to defeat the German invasion of their country in the Second World War, and Stalin himself became a heroic figure. He was even portrayed as a kindly man, with his big moustache and his pipe. But after the war he was able to impose his regime on the countries of eastern Europe which his victorious Red Army had overrun, and his rule became even more repressive.

When he died, Stalin was at first honoured as a great Soviet hero. But soon a new Soviet leader, Nikita Khruschev, exposed some of the terrible things Stalin had done. More recently, other Soviet leaders have given more accounts of his appalling political crimes.

Above *Stalin with other war leaders at the Teheran Conference, at the end of the Second World War. He soon fell out with his wartime allies.*

17
François Duvalier

The countries of Latin America – Central and South America – have suffered under some of the worst political and military tyrants of modern times. The most sinister of all was François Duvalier, who ruled the small Caribbean island republic of Haiti.

He first studied medicine, then he decided to enter politics. Many people admired him for the way he stood up for the poor, underprivileged black population of Haiti, and this helped to get him elected as President. Everybody then expected him to be a liberal ruler. But they were in for a shock.

'Papa Doc', as Duvalier was mockingly called, wanted only riches and power for himself. Very soon his government was being accused of all kinds of bribery and corruption. At the same time, he organized his own secret police force, known as the Ton-Ton-Macoutes (or Bogey Men), who

1907 born in Haiti
1957 elected President of Haiti
1966 his regime condemned by the International Commission of Jurists
1971 dies in office

Right *People at a Voodoo ceremony in 'Papa Doc's' Haiti. He encouraged this primitive form of religion in order to keep the people in a state of ignorance and fear.*

had the power to arrest, torture or execute anyone on his orders.

Worst of all was the way he exploited the ignorance and fears of the poor Haitian population. Many of them practised a form of religion called Voodoo, believing that the power of evil spirits could give them protection or destroy their enemies. Instead of trying to educate the people and rid them of their superstitions, Duvalier declared himself the High Priest of Voodoo, and made sure they were kept in a state of mortal terror.

Finally, he drew up a new Constitution, which made him President for life.

Because of his appalling methods of rule, the United States government stopped all aid to Haiti, and tourists were afraid to go there. Haiti was already a poor, under-developed country, and with no foreign money coming in, life for the islanders became even worse. So it went on, until the death of the terrible 'Papa Doc' in 1971.

Above *François Duvalier pictured with his wife after declaring himself the president of Haiti.*

18
Idi Amin

Some of the worst tyrants of recent times rose to power when Britain and other European countries gave up their empires. One of these was General Idi Amin of Uganda.

Idi Amin Dada Oumee, to give him his full name, had served in the forces of the old British Empire. During the Second World War he fought with the British against the Japanese in Burma, and afterwards joined the King's African Rifles, helping the British in Kenya to fight against the Mau Mau uprising of the 1950s. When Uganda was granted political independence, this huge, tough man (he had also been a boxing champion) used his experience as a soldier to overthrow the government. Amin gave himself the rank of Field Marshal, and as both Commander-in-Chief of the army and President, soon had absolute authority.

Idi Amin tried to appear as a statesman when he became Chairman of the Organization of

1925 born in a village in northern Uganda

1944 serves with the British army in Burma

1946 joins the King's African Rifles and fights for the British in Kenya

1971 overthrows the government of independent Uganda and declares himself President

1975 becomes Chairman of the Organization of African Unity

1979 deposed after invasion by refugee army from Tanzania and flees the country

Right *General Amin watches casually, while his soldiers set fire to a village and slaughter the inhabitants.*

African Unity in 1975. British newspapers, meanwhile, made jokes about his fancy uniforms and titles, and portrayed him as a fool. But the people of Uganda soon gained a different picture of their new ruler. He pursued a policy of racial hatred. He ordered the expulsion of Asians and other foreigners from the country. More dreadful still was his vengeance upon his own people, who happened to belong to tribes that had once been rivals or enemies of his own Kakwa tribe. Refugees fleeing to neighbouring Kenya and Tanzania brought with them terrifying reports of mass murder and torture.

In Uganda itself nobody dared make a move against Amin. But those who had escaped recruited an army and finally invaded Uganda from Tanzania. When they captured the capital of Kampala, Amin fled the country. He took refuge in Libya, swearing to return to Uganda. But he has not done so yet.

Above *Like many tyrants, Idi Amin enjoyed dressing up in military regalia.*

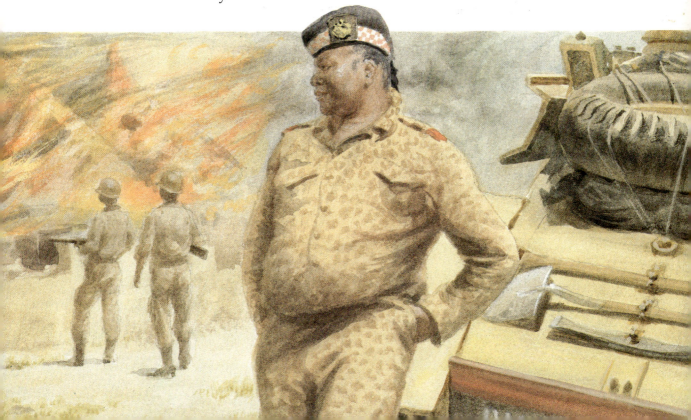

19
Pol Pot

Tyrants often get their chance in times of trouble. This was the case with the man everybody knows as Pol Pot.

His real name was Saloth Sar, and he was born in Kampuchea (formerly Cambodia). He first worked on a rubber plantation, then lived briefly in a monastery, before gaining a scholarship to study as a teacher in France. It was there that he learnt about revolutionary politics. He returned home, took the new name of Pol Pot, and joined the local revolutionary communist movement, called the Khmer Rouge.

The Khmer Rouge planned a new kind of agrarian society for the country, in which everybody worked on the land and lived happily together in villages. Finally, when the Khmer Rouge won political power in 1976, Pol Pot became the Kampuchean leader. He declared the event as 'Year Zero' and the start of a glorious new era.

War with neighbouring Vietnam gave Pol Pot just the chance he wanted. He announced that he was going to evacuate the capital of Phnom Penh and other towns and set up new villages for the people, while his Khmer Rouge soldiers fought a heroic guerilla war against the Vietnamese invaders. This sounded a good idea. But in practice, he forced millions to leave their homes and live in the jungle, where many of them died of starvation or disease. That was not all. Pol Pot's Khmer Rouge troops and police were ordered to kill anyone they suspected of being against the revolution. This included teachers, doctors and other educated people. They were branded as 'intellectual parasites' and were tortured or murdered. It was even dangerous to wear spectacles in Kampuchea at this time – they were regarded as a symbol of Western or intellectual decadence.

Pol Pot and the Khmer Rouge were finally driven from Kampuchea by the Vietnamese army, and the worst of the atrocities were over. But by then perhaps as many as two million helpless men, women and children had died at their hand.

Above *Pol Pot leading a column of his Khmer Rouge troops through the jungle.*

1928	born in Cambodia
1949	studies in Paris
1962	becomes leader of the Khmer Rouge
1976	becomes prime minister of Kampuchea
1979	driven from Kampuchea by the Vietnamese army

Left *Under Pol Pot's orders, Khmer Rouge troops force people to work in the rice paddy fields. They killed anyone they suspected might be against the regime.*

20
Jean Bedel Bokassa

Just as Idi Amin gained power through the ending of British colonial rule, so Jean Bedel Bokassa got his chance when France surrendered her old colonies.

He was born in French Equatorial Africa. Like Amin with the British, he fought in the Free French army during the Second World War, and afterwards fought with French troops in Indo-China (Vietnam), being awarded the Croix de Guerre medal for bravery. Soon after French Equatorial Africa had gained its independence and become the Central African Republic, Colonel Bokassa, as he then was, staged a coup d'etat, and overthrew the government. He dissolved the National Assembly (parliament), declared himself President, and became a dictatorial ruler.

This, however, did not satisfy him for long. Modelling himself on Napoleon Bonaparte, he had

1921 born in French Equatorial Africa
1940 joins the Free French forces in Africa
1954 fights with the French in Indo-China
1966 seizes power in the Central African Republic
1976 crowned Emperor Bokassa I
1979 overthrown and flees the country
1987 faces a second trial over atrocities, sentenced first to death, then to life imprisonment

Right *Bokassa is crowned Emperor on a golden throne. He has bankrupted his country, and has been found guilty of appalling crimes against the people.*

himself crowned Emperor Bokassa I, dressed in robes and shoes of pearls and seated upon a giant gold-plated throne shaped like an eagle. He lived in a marble palace, lit by chandeliers. His wild extravagance ruined the country and he, in turn, was overthrown, fleeing his so-called 'Empire'.

Then terrible stories began to be told about him; how he personally punished enemies and wrong-doers, beating them to death or cutting off their ears. More ghastly still were stories of victims he had fed to his pet lions or crocodiles, and of can-nibalism. Bokassa was put on trial in his absence and sentenced to death. Undeterred, he voluntar-ily returned to his homeland, believing that, like Napoleon after his first period of exile, he would be welcomed back home as a hero. Instead, he was put on trial once more, and again sentenced to death. The new government, though, wanted to show mercy where he had shown none, and reduced the sentence to life imprisonment.

Above *A photograph of Bokassa at his coronation. He soon proved to be a viciously cruel tyrant.*

Glossary

Allies The nations that formed a military alliance against Nazi Germany, Italy and Japan in the Second World War, principally Britain, the United States and the Soviet Union.

Axis The alliance of Germany, Italy and Japan during the Second World War.

Byzantine Relating to the Byzantine Empire, founded by Emperor Constantine I in AD 330.

Censorship The suppression of news or ideas, usually by a government.

Communist Someone who believes in communism – the advocacy of a classless society in which wealth and property is shared by everyone.

Coup d'état The French Team for the illegal, sometimes violent overthrow of a government.

Despot A ruler having almost unlimited power.

Dictator The modern name for a despot.

Fascist A member of a political movement founded by Mussolini, that encouraged militarism and nationalism.

Guerilla A member of an irregular armed force that combats stronger, regular forces.

Heresy Ideas and opinions condemned by the Roman Catholic Church. A person holding such ideas was called a heretic.

Inquisition An institution of the Roman Catholic Church founded to search out and suppress heresy, active between the twelfth and eighteenth centuries.

Inflation Rising prices, which reduce the real value of money.

Legion A large contingent (a division) of soldiers in the Imperial Roman army.

Mausoleum A very large tomb or similar burial place.

Mercenary A soldier who is hired to fight for a foreign army.

Partisans Resistance forces fighting inside occupied territory.

Propaganda The organized spreading of ideas and opinions to assist or damage a government or movement.

Renaissance The period of European history, from about 1400–1600, noted for its art, ideas and discoveries.

Further reading

Borgias, The by David Sweetman (Wayland, 1976)

Boudicca and the Ancient Britons by L. Watson (Wayland, 1986)

Catherine the Great by Miriam Kochan (Wayland, 1976)

Genghis Khan and the Mongols by Andrew Langley (Wayland, 1987)

Hitler by Joshua Rubenstein (Franklin Watts, 1984)

Imperial Rome by Jill Hughes (Hamish Hamilton, 1987)

Italy under Mussolini by Christopher Leeds (Wayland, 1972)

Stalin File, The by Martin McCauley (Batsford, 1979)

Stories of the French Revolution by G. and M. Huisman (Burke Publications, 1984)

Third Reich, The by M. Berwick (Wayland 1971)

Tudors, The by S. L. Case (Bell and Hyman) 1984

Tyrants of the Twentieth Century by Phillip Clark, (Wayland, 1981)

Index

Picture acknowledgements

BBC Hulton Picture Library 11, 19, 23, 33; Camera press 45; Mary Evans Picture Library 21, 29, 31; Hutchison Library 17; Ronald Sheridan 13, 27; Richard Sharpley 7; Topham Picture Library 35, 37, 39, 41, 43; Wayland Picture Library 25.